Paris

For my mother

Jan Hess

Thank you for being the most wonderful mother in the entire world.
I love you to the top of the Eiffel Tower and back.

Paris

—

THROUGH A FASHION EYE

Megan Hess

hardie grant books

Contents

Introduction

—

I was completely in love with Paris long before I set foot in France. As a little girl, I dreamt of every Parisian cliche – climbing the Eiffel Tower, riding a bicycle through the cobblestone streets and, of course, eating baguettes and pastries for breakfast, lunch and dinner.

When I eventually travelled to Paris in my early twenties, it was everything I had dreamt of. I was completely penniless at the time, but I still felt like every experience in the city was incredible. I remember sitting in the beautiful Tuileries, eating an icecream and wondering if my life would one day bring me to work in this romantic city. To my absolute joy, it did!

One of my first big commissions was for Cartier. The brief was to illustrate their Paris Nouvelle Vague collection and they asked me to make sure I took time to see all that was beautiful before rushing in to illustrate the pieces – it's a metaphor for life and something I have never forgotten. It also made me truly understand how incredibly detailed and passionate Parisians are.

Since then I have been very privileged to work with many other incredible iconic French luxury brands, such as Dior, Louis Vuitton, Chanel and Le Bristol Paris. Paris has become an enormous source of inspiration for my work since becoming fashion illustrator. Throughout the year I travel back and forth to Paris, and I only have to glimpse a tiny iron balcony with a signature flower pot of French roses to go completely weak at the knees. I have acquired a hefty list of my favourite fashion places, to eat, shop and explore. From dining at Paris's finest restaurants with Baccarat Crystal to finding the tiny unassuming bistros, there are so many wonderful Parisian experiences. The shopping is incredible, whether you're at the couture houses or at the eclectic flea markets looking for bargain treasures.

And in addition to all that Paris has to offer to a fashion-lover like myself, I think the people-watching is second to none. My favourite spot is at Café de Flore – I love sitting at a cosy table, sipping an espresso and sketching all the wonderful French fashion that passes me by. I hope this guide helps you find your favourite spot to fall in love with and experience the beauty that is Paris!

My favourite things ...

Dior Luggage

Chanel Bag

Large Sketch Book

Travel Diary

Cartier Scarf

Sunglasses

Fedora

... to pack for Paris

Boots, Heels

Killer Boots

PEONIES
THE ROSE GARDEN
VALENTINO

COCO
MADEMOISELLE
CHANEL
PARIS

Coco Scent

Pink Lips

Party Dress

Shopping Bag

Dior Slippers

Hermès Bangles

My favourite ensembles ...

WE SHOULD ALL BE FEMINISTS

J'ADIOR

Dinner & Cocktails

Shopping on Rue Cambon

Going to the Opera

... for Paris occasions

Exploring
St Germain

Coffee with
Karl Lagerfeld

Fashion Week Gala

01

Do/
Play

Saint-Germain-des-Prés

6E

Surrounded by Paris's Latin Quarter (the fifth arrondissement and home to Sorbonne University), Jardin du Luxembourg and the Left Bank of the Seine, Saint-Germain-des-Prés is steeped in cultural history. Its winding bohemian streets were a favourite haunt of great writers and thinkers including Ernest Hemingway, Jean-Paul Sartre and Simone de Beauvoir. Today the area is a vibrant fashion and art strip. It is full of luxury boutiques and galleries like the modernist art institution Cahiers d'Art, which was founded in 1926 and championed the early works of Marcel Duchamp, Man Ray and Joan Miró. When you're weary of wandering the area's cultural offerings, you should step into my favourite cafe in Paris, Café de Flore, on boulevard Saint-Germain. It is one of the oldest and most iconic coffee houses in Paris (Picasso was one of its many notable patrons) and it's the best place to sit back with your coffee of choice and enjoy the age-old pastime of people-watching.

GALLERY

19

Dior Institut au Plaza Athénée

25 AVENUE MONTAIGNE,
8E

The Dior Institut au Plaza Athénée delivers a spa experience of haute couture standards. It neighbours Christian Dior's original atelier at 30 avenue Montaigne (*see page 66*) – the address where the couturier launched his iconic 'New Look' collection in 1947 and heralded a new era of femininity. Paying homage to its namesake, the walls of the Dior Institut bear the distinctive 'CD' logo set against muted tones of cream and white, in an environment of tranquil luxury. Spend the day relaxing with treatments from the spa menu developed by the Dior beauty team. The treatments on offer honour the couturier's love of fragrant flora with ingredients like rose de Granville, which is grown exclusively in the Dior garden in Grasse (*see page 56*).

Pont Alexandre III

I consider this the prettiest bridge in the entire world! A pair of winged gilt bronze statues greets visitors at either end of the Pont Alexandre III, the ornate Beaux-Arts style bridge that links Paris's Rive Gauche (Left Bank) with the Rive Droite (Right Bank) across the Seine. A historic landmark, the bridge was built in 1900 for the World Fair – Exposition Universelle – hosted in Paris that year. The golden statues at either end of the bridge symbolise the arts, science, commerce and industry. A stroll across the bridge affords stunning views of the Eiffel Tower. It is a beautiful, romantic setting and fittingly features in Woody Allen's mystical film *Midnight in Paris*.

23

Le Marais

3E AND 4E

Translating into English as 'the marsh', Paris's Le Marais may have started out as a marsh but it has been many things since then. Early on it was an aristocratic neighbourhood, then it became a commercial centre, a working-class district and today it's buzzing with a new energy as an artistic and sartorial precinct, renowned for its edgy art,

fashion and night-life. Spread over the city's third and fourth arrondissements, the area now attracts a hip crowd with its selection of concept stores, boutique bars and high-end galleries. During Paris Fashion Week Le Marais buzzes with glamorous excitement, as the designers' press offices and showrooms bring the high fashion set to its winding streets.

Eiffel Tower

CHAMP DE MARS, 5 AVENUE
ANATOLE, 7E

I've lost count of how many times I have drawn the Eiffel Tower over the years. Nothing is more symbolic of the City of Lights than its beloved Tour Eiffel. The structure was designed and built by engineer Gustave Eiffel in 1889, and has been a subject of fascination for artists and photographers ever since. The elegant, lofty form of the tower captured the imagination of fashion photographer Erwin Blumenfeld, who famously photographed model Lisa Fonssagrives precariously poised on its edge, her gown billowing in the wind, for *Vogue* in 1939. The ever-irreverent designer Jean-Paul Gaultier has also used the symbol of the Eiffel Tower throughout his collections, from featuring the motif in lace stockings to mimicking the metal latticework in the frame of sunglasses. Replicated time and again, the Eiffel Tower is one of the most iconic buildings of the modern era.

Palais Garnier

8 RUE SCRIBE, 9E

The grand building of the Palais Garnier is one of Paris's most breathtaking sights. It is located at the top of avenue de l'Opéra, and walking up its wide steps into the ornate arches of its majestic facade feels like a moment of theatre in itself. The domed neo-baroque building was unveiled in 1867 as part of Baron Haussmann's vision for urban Paris, and it remains the home of the city's theatre and opera activities. Inside, the building is every bit as stunning as its facade, with each of the spaces reflecting Paris's historical opulence. In the grand auditorium an awe-inspiring seven-ton bronze and crystal candelabra hangs against the backdrop of a ceiling painted by the modernist artist Marc Chagall in 1964. Truly a sight to behold!

Ritz Club
Paris

17 PLACE VENDÔME, 1ER

Since it opened in 1989, the Ritz Club Paris – the spa at the exclusive hotel – has been the destination of choice for the fashion set. During Paris Fashion Week, they come here to unwind after a frantic day of shows. In 2012 the hotel underwent major renovations. Four years later it re-opened with the exciting addition of Chanel au Ritz Paris to its spa offering. The spa pays homage to Coco Chanel – who resided in a private suite at The Ritz for years – in every detail, from

the beige-and-black colour scheme to the Chanel beauty products that line the shelves of the entrance area. After treating yourself from the menu of indulgent pampering sessions, take a dip in the club's stunning pool of azure-blue water lined with thousands of small blue tiles and live that important Chanel principle of 'luxury for yourself'. Personally, I like to imagine Coco here today getting a pedicure – beige nail polish of course!

Moulin Rouge

82 BOULEVARD DE CLICHY, 18E

An extravagant whirl of colour, music, feathers, sequins, rhinestones, cartwheels and incredible dancing, a Moulin Rouge performance is truly a spectacle for the senses.

When it first opened in 1889, the Moulin Rouge was touted as 'a temple of music and dance', but instead it gained a reputation for being a naughty establishment where ladies with lithe limbs and loose morals performed the can-can – among other things – for the entertainment of men.

These days it's a much more refined affair and many notable artists – including Edith Piaf, Elton John, Frank Sinatra and Ella Fitzgerald – have graced the Moulin Rouge stage.

33

rue Saint-Honoré

1ER

S aint-Honoré is a veritable feast for the fashion inclined. Running parallel to rue de Rivoli (which is home to the Louvre), Saint-Honoré manages to avoid the tourist hustle and bustle. One of the street's most popular destinations, Colette, the tongue-in-cheek high-end fashion market and gallery, is a must. Enjoy the playful, ever-changing window displays before venturing in to admire the designer fashions. The street is also home to a handful of fantastic vintage jewellery boutiques, such as Lydia Courteille and Dary's. Rue Saint-Honoré is also one of my favourite places for people-watching, as Paris's well-heeled make their way from boutique to boutique.

Arc de Triomphe

Standing tall at the intersection of several converging streets, the breathtaking Arc de Triomphe is located in place Charles de Gaulle (also known as place de l'Étoile) where the Champs-Élysées meets avenue Matignon and avenue Franklin Delano Roosevelt. The grand arch, at nearly fifty metres high, was commissioned in 1806 by the emperor Napoleon Bonaparte to celebrate his victory at Austerlitz. The structure houses the underground Tomb of the Unknown Soldier, a memorial to lives lost in the First World War. The regal boulevards leading to the Arc de Triomphe, and beyond avenue Foch into the gardens of Bois de Boulogne, reflect Paris at its best: elegant, soaring grandeur. I recommend taking the stairs to the very top at sunset – it's one of my favourite views of Paris.

Carousel rides

VARIOUS LOCATIONS

The fairytale image of a rotating carousel is quintessential Paris at Christmas. During winter, carousels emerge at various sites throughout the city. Their merry-go-round music floats through the streets and the city's jardins. Temporary and permanent carousel rides dotted throughout the city – including at Hôtel de Ville, the Jardin des Tuileries and the base of the Eiffel Tower – evoke old-world Parisian charm and transform Paris into a playground. The rides are such a Parisian motif that, for its spring/summer 2012 collection, Louis Vuitton recreated a shimmering white carousel in the Louvre's Cour Carrée where the seasonal shows are held. Decked out in candy colours and fine broderie anglaise, the models encircled the fairground ride before strutting down the runway.

Musée du Louvre and Musée de la Mode et du Textile

RUE DE RIVOLI, 1ER

A trip to Paris would be incomplete without a visit to the Louvre. One of the most revered art institutions in the world, the building itself dates back to the late twelfth century. It has seen a trajectory from fortress, to seat of power, to one of the most visited art museums in the world today. The lofty palace wraps around a courtyard with a stunning glass pyramid in the middle that leads visitors underground and into the museum. The Louvre houses some of the most important works of art and decorative objects from history, including the *Winged Victory of Samothrace* and Da Vinci's enigmatic *Mona Lisa*. But for any fashion connoisseur, a visit to the Musée de la Mode et du Textile (a department of the Musée des Arts Décoratifs) is a must. Located in the western wing of the Louvre (but separate from it, so you'll need to pay admission), the collection boasts over 150,000 works ranging from costumes to accessories to textiles, and has hosted fashion exhibitions featuring Dries Van Noten, Louis Vuitton, Marc Jacobs and Madeleine Vionnet. Just remember – you need more than a day to cover it all so plan out exactly what you want to see.

Coco Chanel's apartment

31 RUE CAMBON, 1ER

Coco Chanel's name and style have been synonymous with rue Cambon since 1910 when the designer opened her millinery shop at number 21. Later she moved a few doors down to number 31, which would become the most iconic address for Chanel, both the woman and the brand.

In the centre of the building is a faceted, mirrored staircase, where the great couturier would perch at the top to look over her designs from every angle as the models moved up and down the stairs. The staircase links the ground floor to the salons above – the exclusive locale for haute couture fittings with celebrities and loyal clientele.

While tours of the apartment are by special appointment only, the retail store on the ground floor is a wonderful place to visit. There you'll find all of the classics – the quilted 2.55 bag, the beige-and-black two-tone pumps and the inimitable Chanel No. 5 scent – in which Chanel's vision still lives on.

COCO CHANEL

Paris Fashion Week at the Jardin des Tuileries

PLACE DE LA CONCORDE, 1ER

The city transforms for Paris Fashion Week, a mainstay of French culture, when the fashion set takes over to showcase the best designers in the world. The busy schedule of men's, women's and haute couture fashion events is organised by the Fédération Française de la Couture du Prêt-à-Porter des

Couturiers et des Créateurs de Mode. With women's ready-to-wear collections shown each February and September, the heart of the action takes place at the Jardin des Tuileries, a stone's throw from the Louvre and the city centre. Here, as well as at various off-site locations, high fashion design houses like Yves Saint Laurent, Dior, Rick Owens and Lanvin parade their artistry. Whether you can get your hands on an invite to rub shoulders with the influencers, models and magazine editors, or people-watch from afar, it's hard to avoid the thrill of fashion week.

Grand Palais

AVENUE WINSTON CHURCHILL, 8E

A landmark of modern Paris, the Grand Palais extends a breathtaking 240 metres across the eighth arrondissement at the east end of the Champs-Élysées.

The soaring glass-and-steel-domed structure was built in 1900 for Paris's World Fair, and continues to be used as a venue for exhibitions and events hosted by the city.

Each season the Grand Palais comes alive during the Paris Fashion Week as the venue of choice for Chanel's theatrical fashion shows. Karl Lagerfeld's elaborate catwalks never cease to amaze. In the past he's created an epic winter setting with an iceberg shipped from Sweden, a Chanel Brasserie and even a giant Chanel jacket. With grand creations like that, Lagerfeld's show is the most anticipated event of every fashion week.

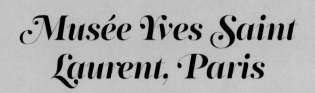

Musée Yves Saint Laurent, Paris

5 AVENUE MARCEAU, 16E

—

From the safari suit to 'Le Smoking', Yves Saint Laurent revolutionised fashion since first setting up his eponymous fashion house in 1961. After working for the great Christian Dior, Saint Laurent, together with his partner Pierre Bergé, created haute couture and prêt-à-porter that would shape Paris fashion. The Fondation Pierre Bergé–Yves Saint Laurent, an organisation set up in 2004 to honour the designer's legacy, opened this museum in 2017 within the original atelier of the fashion house, on avenue Marceau. With an archive of over 5000 of Yves Saint Laurent's garments, rotating exhibition displays will be presented in the unique setting. Surrounded by the designer's sketches, personal artifacts and working tools, the museum offers us style lovers a rare and inspiring glimpse into one of the great minds of twentieth-century fashion.

Grand Musée du Parfum

73 RUE DU FAUBOURG
SAINT-HONORÉ, 8E

French fragrances and high fashion go hand-in-hand, and Le Grand Musée du Parfum is a must for any fragrance-lover. This carefully curated scent-centred museum will have you following your nose through history, from ancient Egyptian times, when the woody smells of Kyphi were used to call on the gods, through to the modern era, in which intricate science experiments give birth to finely tuned perfumes. Fittingly set within a nineteenth-century mansion, this sensory journey reveals all there is to know about the revered, mystical substance that is French perfume.

·Do/Play

Beyond Paris

Château de Versailles

One of the most breathtaking destinations, the Château de Versailles and its surrounding grounds continue to attract a stream of visitors each year. Originally a royal hunting lodge for Louis XIII, his successor Louis XIV transformed the site into an epic palace, moving the court of France to reside at Versailles in 1682. The site later became home to Louis XVI and his wife, the Austrian princess Marie-Antoinette, one of history's most infamous fashion icons. A short train journey from Paris, the palace is listed as a World Heritage Site and is nothing short of awe-inspiring. Barely an inch of the interior has been spared from gilding or lavish baroque and neo-classical ornamentation. From the King's grand apartments to Marie-Antoinette's quaint playground and estate, the Petit Trianon, Versailles is an architectural feast. The Hall of Mirrors, which served as a place for courtiers and visitors to meet and was also a venue for important ceremonies, is spectacular. Lined with 357 mirrors – objects that at the time were considered to be the height of luxury – the soaring passageway is truly reminiscent of a fairytale setting.

VER

ILLES

Château de La Colle Noire

220 ROUTE
DÉPARTEMENTALE 562,
MONTAUROUX

Offering a retreat for the great couturier, Christian Dior's Château de La Colle Noir is an idyllic fifteenth-century chateau that was bought by the designer in 1951. It was sold not long after Dior died in 1957. The House of Dior purchased the property once again in 2013, renovating it as a new home for the house's fragrances. Painstakingly restored, complete with cream wallpaper and silk drapery, the rooms of the house and surrounding gardens reflect a more private side of the designer but remain true to his love of pure, classic luxury. The chateau and surrounding gardens are set in the rolling hills of Montauroux,

a village near Grasse, and are filled with
fragrant flora reflecting Dior's love of nature
and its scents. As the designer once said, 'After
women, flowers are the most lovely thing God
has given the world.'

Musée Christian Dior

1 RUE D'ESTOUTEVILLE,
GRANVILLE

H ome to a vast collection of the couturier's sartorial creations, the pale pink Musée Christian Dior is the dedicated museum of Dior. Set in Villa les Rhumbs, Dior's childhood home in Granville, in the region of Normandy, the museum was created at the property in 1997. A seasonal schedule of exhibitions showcases the vast and varied output of the designer and the House of Dior. From his love of flora, a theme of both his haute couture designs and fragrances, to his iconic 'New Look' collection of 1947, Dior's legacy to twentieth-century fashion is made available for public view. The journey north beyond Paris to the museum is a must for any fashion devotee.

Champagne, wine region

NORTH-EAST FRANCE

Drinking bubbles from a lady's slipper is said to have been a habit for Parisian bourgeoisie during the Belle Époque; these days a fashion party is incomplete without a steady flow of Champagne. Escape Paris with a daytrip to where it all began: the World Heritage–listed region that is home to the many wineries that create Champagne. From boutique winemakers to iconic brands like Moët & Chandon and Veuve Clicquot, Champagne is home to over 15,000 wine growers. A visit to Hautvillers is a must; the small village is credited as the birthplace of bubbles and as the place where the Benedictine monk Dom Pierre Pérignon is said to have invented Champagne. It's no secret that Champagne and fashion go hand in hand – so much so, that designer Jean-Paul Gaultier has collaborated to design a lace-corsetted bottle for Piper-Heidsieck.

02

Shop

Chanel

31 RUE CAMBON, 1ER

After opening her hat boutique on rue Cambon in 1910, Mademoiselle Chanel made a name for herself as the Grand Dame of French couture; she would change the way women dressed forever. Her name became synonymous with modern, luxury dressing. Now Karl Lagerfeld continues that tradition while guiding Chanel into the twenty-first century. He continues to reinvent Chanel classics with his own irreverent humour. One of several of the brand's boutiques that call Paris home occupies the ground floor of the Chanel flagship at 31 rue Cambon. The eighteenth-century building also houses Coco's apartment and was where the exclusive salon shows were originally held. The store downstairs at number 31 is every bit Chanel and my favourite place to shop in all of Paris!

31

CHANEL

Paris!

Dior

Ever since launching his 1947 'New Look' collection, Christian Dior has been a name synonymous with haute couture. Dior moved into the avenue Montaigne a year earlier. The historic premises is where the house's collections continue to be imagined today, ensuring that the Dior name lives on as a global brand. The ateliers on the upper levels of the building have seen some of the biggest names in fashion reinvent the brand, from John Galliano to Raf Simons and now Maria Grazia Chiuri. One of my most thrilling commissions was sketching live for Dior Couture. Discover where it all began at the flagship store that has been transformed by luxury retail guru Peter Marino. Marino's refurbishment decorated the eighteenth-century interior with contemporary details, paying homage to the couturier's original vision of classic luxury.

Louis Vuitton

101 AVENUE DES CHAMPS-ÉLYSÉES, 8E

Over the years I have sketched many times for Louis Vuitton, from bags to shoes to their iconic trunks. Since Louis Vuitton opened up shop as a luggage maker in 1854, his name has dominated luxury fashion. The Louis Vuitton flagship store, standing tall at number 101 on the grand avenue des Champs-Élysées, stocks all things LV from the monogrammed luggage to the latest collections created by artistic director Nicolas Ghesquière. Since he joined the house in 2013, Ghesquière has brought a visionary approach to womenswear. The classic LV logo of the global brand, which is now owned by the LVMH (Moët Hennessy Louis Vuitton) group, emblazoned on brown leather remains the brand's hallmark. So much so that to celebrate its 150th anniversary in 2004, the store's facade was literally encased in a giant Louis Vuitton brown leather trunk.

Givenchy

36 AVENUE MONTAIGNE, 8E

The man behind Audrey Hepburn's iconic outfits for the 1961 film *Breakfast at Tiffany's*, Paris couturier Hubert de Givenchy, brought the Little Black Dress into the fashion vernacular. Although he was dressing chic and glamorous women and fashion icons like Jackie Kennedy and Grace Kelly, Hepburn was an exceptional muse for Givenchy. He designed many of the actress's most well-known ensembles on and off the screen. Today, in the hands of Clare Waight Keller, the house of Givenchy remains a cornerstone of fashion.

Appointed in May 2017 as Givenchy's first female artistic director, Keller featured both menswear and womenswear in her elegant but seductive debut collection. Givenchy's Parisian home on avenue Montaigne in the eighth arrondissement honours the legacy of Hubert de Givenchy. Architect Joseph Dirand led the conversion of the historic building and used raw materials, including marble and steel, in a sleek way to create the ultimate air of sophistication. It is the perfect showcase for Keller's creations.

BALMAIN
PARIS

Balmain

44 RUE FRANÇOIS 1ER, 8E

Dressing some of Paris's most loved muses, such as Josephine Baker and Brigitte Bardot, Balmain is an establishment in Paris's high fashion scene. With Olivier Rousteing now at the helm, the house has garnered a cult following of celebrities and the fashion inclined. Renovated in 2009, by architect and decorator Joseph Dirand, Balmain's flagship boutique at 44 rue François 1er honours the house's heritage and the discreet, classic luxury that Pierre Balmain cultivated. Parquetry floors and white-panelled walls serve as an austere backdrop to Rousteing's designs, which favour a monochromatic palette of black and white with flashes of gold.

Lanvin

15 AND 22 RUE DU
FAUBOURG
SAINT-HONORÉ,
8E

Emerging from the Art Deco period, Jeanne Lanvin made a name for herself with the glamorous cocktail frocks of the Roaring Twenties. Lanvin lives on as a global brand, with its playful glamour expanding to menswear, accessories and a range of fragrances. In recent years the house has seen designers Alber Elbaz and now Bouchra Jarrar bring their own vision to the label's tradition of sumptuous, high fashion eveningwear. Nestled in amongst the other luxury boutiques in the designer district, Lanvin's men's and women's flagship stores at 15 and 22 rue du Faubourg Saint-Honoré attract devout Parisian and international followers.

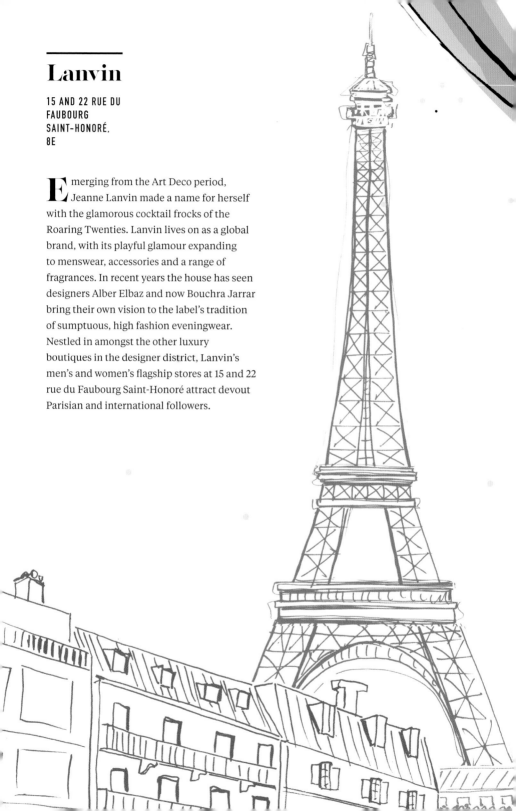

Hermès

24 RUE DU FAUBOURG
SAINT-HONORÉ, 8E

Founded in 1837 as suppliers of equestrian accessories to members of high society, the French luxury house Hermès is steeped in history. These days the global brand is more famed for its line of luxury accessories, womenswear and menswear. The Hermès ready-to-wear lines are overseen by designers Nadège Vanhee-Cybulski (womenswear) and Véronique Nichanian (menswear). Two women at the helm

is a rare occurence within the male-dominated fashion industry. The flagship, a multi-level boutique at 24 rue du Faubourg Saint-Honoré, delivers all things Hermès amid the eighth arrondissement's hive of luxury fashion. Clothing, luggage and accessories – including the iconic silk scarves – all leave the store in the brand's famous orange packaging.

Christian Louboutin

**17 AND 19 RUE JEAN–
JACQUES ROUSSEAU, 1ER**

Parisian sole designer Christian Louboutin has been inspiring shoe fetishes since he set up shop in 1991. One of his most iconic designs – the trademarked red-soled stiletto – may reference the designer's French roots in an ode to Louis XIV's red heels and the sumptuary codes of the baroque period. A versatile designer, Louboutin manages to be anywhere and everywhere, from presenting in-store exhibitions to creating his own iPhone app to designing the uniforms worn by Cuban athletes for the 2016 Olympic Games in Rio de Janeiro. With a chic following at home and abroad, Louboutin's Parisian stores on rue Jean-Jacques Rousseau place the men's and women's boutiques side by side, each complete with Louboutin's signature lipstick red carpet underfoot.

Comme des Garçons

54 RUE DU FAUBOURG
SAINT-HONORÉ, 8E

When the avant-garde Japanese designers, including Comme des Garçons' Rei Kawakubo, descended on Paris Fashion Week in the early 1980s their presence caused a stir. Designer and founder Kawakubo's anti-fashion silhouettes defied beauty standards and brought about a new era in womenswear. From deconstructed jackets to dresses containing lumps and bumps, Kawakubo keeps her place in haute couture as the boundary-pushing designer and retailer. Comme des Garçons stores are now spread across major cities, selling its extravagant high fashion pieces and its more street-oriented Play label. The brand's flagship Paris store lures devout Comme followers through an unassuming doorway that leads into an off-street courtyard where a gallery-like setting, designed by French studio ARTIS, stocks some of their more groundbreaking catwalk creations.

COMME des GARÇONS
*

Isabel Marant

1 RUE JACOB, 6E

W ell known for her design of the heeled sneaker –
the shoe that has been strutting streets from Paris
to Shanghai – Isabel Marant has been making a name for
herself in quirky-but-feminine womenswear since starting out
in 1995. After dipping her toes in, working for other brands
in the fashion industry, Marant launched her eponymous
label, using friends as models for her first collection, which
she set in the courtyard of a Paris squat. The designer is now
stocked worldwide, as well as having twenty-two Isabel Marant

boutiques around the globe (four of which call Paris home), garnering a loyal following of her wearable designs. Each season Isabel Marant collaborates with ceramicist, designer and sculptor Arnold Goron on the window displays of her retail settings; even in this detail she remains faithful to her passion for handmade creations.

Saint
Laurent

6 PLACE SAINT-SULPICE,
6E

Y ves Saint Laurent is a name that is intricately woven into
the fabric of Paris high fashion. The brand has moved
effortlessly through its various iterations: from pioneering
ready-to-wear clothes, to nightclub chic with Tom Ford, to
the moody, skinny suit silhouette of Hedi Slimane. Slimane,
who rebranded the house to simply Saint Laurent, honoured
1970s late night, rock-star glamour with collections of tailored

silhouettes, leather jackets and skinny denim. He was replaced as creative director
in 2016 by Anthony Vacarello, who continues to bring out the darker side of Saint Laurent.
The luxury house's flagship store resides on place Saint-Sulpice in the sixth arrondissement.
The boutique, which first opened in 1979, reflects the Saint Laurent trajectory from past to
present. Overlooking the historic church of Église Saint-Sulpice, the store opens into
a monochromatic interior featuring white marble floors and mirrored metal fixtures,
the perfect setting for the sleek ready-to-wear garments fresh off the runway.

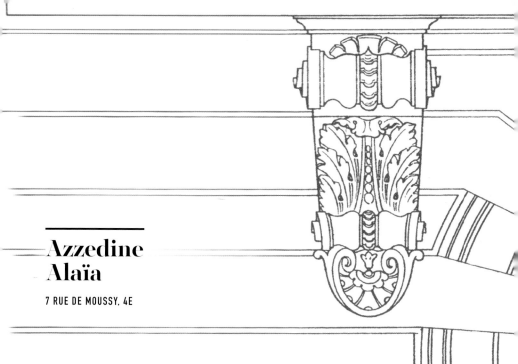

Azzedine Alaïa

7 RUE DE MOUSSY, 4E

Nicknamed by the media as the 'king of cling', Tunisian-born, Paris-based designer Azzedine Alaïa has been outfitting women since the heyday of the supermodel. Wrapping icons from Grace Jones to Madonna in his signature figure-hugging bandage dresses, Alaïa's work as a seminal designer was honoured in 2013 in a retrospective at the Palais Galliera's Musée de la mode de la Ville de Paris. Alaïa's seasonal ready-to-wear lines can be found in his Parisian boutiques, which display the designer's masterful skill in cut and form, showcasing dresses as works of art. The designer's location at 7 rue de Moussy is truly worth a visit and is also home to the brand's office and studio. The boutique downstairs is every bit as avant-garde as the clothing and features a stunning Carrara marble room designed by Marc Newson, which displays the shoe collection. You may struggle to find an occasion for Alaïa's figure-sculpting bandage dresses and killer heels, but the store itself is a sight to behold.

·Repetto

22 RUE DE LA PAIX, 2E

—

Amidst rows of endless variations on the ballet flat, it's easy to see why Repetto has become the go-to shop for off-duty ballerinas and the fashion savvy. Its second arrondissement store on rue de la Paix is an ode to the shoe, providing a welcome alternative to the towering heels flogged by the designer boutiques in this luxury district. Rose Repetto founded the company in 1947 and opened her first store at rue de la Paix in 1959. The brand has since become a favourite of the fashion crowd from Brigitte Bardot to Karlie Kloss. Repetto shoes continue to stand out in front, featuring product collaborations with fashion icons like Issey Miyake and Karl Lagerfeld. The brand even branched out into fragrance, launching the Repetto 'Eau de Toilette' in 2014. As well as the soft ballet shoe, the store houses the label's ballet wear and ready-to-wear collections. At least we can all look as graceful as a ballerina.

colette:

Colette

213 RUE
SAINT-HONORÉ,
1ER

The uber cool Colette has been drawing fashion devotees in a steady stream ever since it opened in 1997. The trailblazing boutique has become a template for the concept store with several levels covering all things art, music and fashion. The ground floor of the corner building carries a rotating mix of streetwear, accessories and publications – it's always a thrill to see my books stocked on their coveted table space. Stairs take customers up to the first floor, which houses a curated range of cutting-edge fashion. The basement is home to a gallery space and the Water Bar (with a menu of over 100 varieties of bottled water, sourced globally) that refreshes the Colette faithful after wandering the store – it's hard work, but worth it! The show is run by retail impresario Sarah Lerfel, who sets a fast pace of collaborations, launches and events, as well as a rotating window display, all of which keep Colette at the fore of luxury.

Galeries Lafayette

**40 BOULEVARD
HAUSSMANN, 9E**

Since opening as a small haberdashery store in 1893, Galeries Lafayette has grown into a retail empire, earning the title of 'luxury bazaar'. Enter the Paris flagship on boulevard Haussmann to a circular multi-level floor plan that leads shoppers around the outskirts of the central space, which is lit up by an Art Nouveau stained-glass domed ceiling.

The store's magical interior, from the ornate scalloped
arches at the dome's edges to the gilt and wrought iron
balconies on each level, will transport you to another
era – Paris at the turn of the nineteenth century. Start with
the extensive beauty department on the ground floor, then
ascend to the curated selection of designer fashion, books,
homewares and accessories on the upper levels that make
Galeries Lafayette a must for Paris shopping.

diptyque

paris

Diptyque

34 BOULEVARD SAINT-GERMAIN, 5E

The status of a Diptyque candle is akin to the coffee table book: its unmistakable oval graphic labels are coveted in home settings. The candle makers have been in business since 1961 when three creative friends, Christiane Gautrot (an interior decorator), Desmond Knox-Leet (a painter) and Yves Coueslant (a set designer), opened their boutique at 34 boulevard Saint-Germain. The corner-store boutique, with its maroon facade emblazoned with gold script spelling out 'Diptyque', embodies a luxury apothecary. The interior reflects a cosy and ecclectic mix of heritage references, with liberty-patterned wallpaper and carved wood fixtures that house rows of the luxe candles. Diptyque do not classify its range of candles, fragrances, body products and skincare as either masculine or feminine; instead it allows the raw ingredients to speak for themselves and to you.

Cartier

154 AVENUE DES
CHAMPS-ÉLYSÉES,
8E

Cartier's luxury pieces have draped the necks of the royal dynasties, from Princess Marie Bonaparte to the Duke and Duchess of Windsor to the inimitable Grace Kelly. Starting out in the business of jewels and watches in 1847, the house that Louis Cartier founded now has over 200 stores across the world. The emblem of the panther – created by Jeanne Toussaint, Cartier's muse and creative director of jewellery from 1933 until 1970 –

remains a hallmark of the house, appearing on brooches and neck pieces. Since opening in 2015, the new Cartier flagship store on the Champs-Élysées has become a destination for luxury shoppers. Designed by regular collaborator architect Bruno Moinard, the store is a stunning temple to all things Cartier, reflecting the timeless elegance at the heart of Cartier. Several years ago I illustrated for Cartier's Paris Nouvelle Vague collection during Fashion Week. Seeing and sketching its incredible pieces was one of my favourite commissions.

Merci

111 BOULEVARD BEAUMARCHAIS, 3E

Entering through a courtyard into the store's lofty concept space, customers are immediately confronted by Merci's signature quirky take on Parisian style. The boutique's curated range of homewares, clothing and publications are displayed in different spaces throughout the building with typical off-beat Merci merchandising. Since it was founded by Bernard and Marie-France Cohen in 2009, Merci has made its name through its eclectic approach to retail, mixing elements and references from global crafts to high art with joie de vivre. When you're ready for a break from browsing Merci's intriguing mix of wares, take a seat and order some sustenance at the shop's delightful café nestled in the courtyard.

99

Chloé

Chloé

253 RUE SAINT-HONORÉ, 1ER

I always imagine the Chloé girl floating through the Tuileries in one of Chloé's signature romantic, ethereal dresses. Founded in 1952 by Gaby Aghion, the house of Chloé continues to bring its relaxed and youthful feminine aesthetic to the ready-to-wear table. Embracing its youthful ideal, the brand has historically supported young talent including Karl Lagerfeld and Stella McCartney, both of whom have enjoyed success at its helm. Natacha Ramsay-Levi now heads the house as its creative director, and the label continues to amass a global following. Chloé's flagship store on rue Saint-Honoré is chic luxury. Set in the designer district of the first arrondissement, the store's stunning setting was created by interior architect guru Joseph Dirand and is a space of soft white-washed simplicity; clean lines, from the shelving to the white marble counter areas, are highlighted by gold detailing. A mustard yellow sofa adds a splash of colour to the ground floor space, which flows into an elegant curved staircase beckoning the shopper to continue their dream-like journey into the romantic, free-spirited world of Chloé.

Karl Lagerfeld

25 RUE VIEILLE DU TEMPLE, 4E

The inimitable Karl Lagerfeld continues to reign over high fashion, creating countless collections as well as running his own label, co-designing Fendi and being the creative director of Chanel. The Karl Lagerfeld store in Le Marais reflects a youthful, street-savvy setting, but still resonates with the designer's quintessential wit and irreverence when it comes to all things fashion. The black facade of the boutique is adorned with the Lagerfeld logo – a black and white profile

of the designer sporting his unmistakable ponytail and black sunglasses. Step inside and you'll find the range of leather bags, accessories and ready-to-wear clothes. You can even take home your very own Karl Lagerfeld doll. Obviously, I have several!

Chantal Thomass

211 RUE SAINT-HONORÉ, 1ER

If there was ever a place to revive your lingerie drawer, this would be it! Enter the glitzy boudoir of Chantal Thomass through the brand's decadent rue Saint-Honoré flagship. Thomass takes Parisian chic to the next level and has made a name for herself with hosiery and lingerie that reaches the height of femininity. From fishnet stockings to fine lace knickers and Swarovski-encrusted bodysuits, the brand's seductive lingerie pieces are designed to be worn with little else. Thomass, who founded the company in 1975, remains at the helm and oversees its regular collaborations. Whether it's art directing a show at the Parisian cabaret institution Crazy Horse, or creating her own signature version of the French éclair for patisserie and dessert supplier Fauchon, Thomass never ceases to delight her devotees.

Annick Goutal

16 RUE DE BELLECHASSE, 7E

Ever since it opened the rue de Bellechasse boutique, Annick Goutal's luxury fragrance house has been attracting scent enthusiasts from around the globe. Passion for raw materials remains the cornerstone of any Goutal scent; its range honours natural ingredients like Sicilian lemon, Damascus rose and tuberose from Grasse. Fragrances with names like 'Un Matin d'Orage' and 'Tenue de Soirée' reflect the kind of sophistication and luxury embodied by the house. Having branched out into body and skincare ranges and scented candles, its stores are as luxurious as the products for sale. The rue de Bellechasse store reflects the brand's Parisian roots with its playful rotating window displays, eclectic interior design, and the decorative perfume bottles that hold the Goutal fragrances. A bottle of Annick is the perfect keepsake to bring back from your travels.

Guerlain

68 AVENUE DES
CHAMPS-ÉLYSÉES, 8E

L a maison Guerlain sits pretty as a picture on the Champs-Élysées, its cursive script decorating the facade underneath the arches of the historic building. The heritage brand has been in the business of perfume for more than 185 years, and the store at number 68 is a destination for fragrance lovers, attracting Guerlain loyalists and tourists alike. Featuring mirrored walls, Murano crystal chandeliers and grand marble-lined spaces, the retail bazaar's interior was designed by luxury retail guru Peter Marino. Guerlain's fragrance, skincare and makeup ranges fill the sections of the store, each of which has a unique and distinctively boutique feel. The fragrance room upstairs features a sculptural perfume display, lined with bottles of Guerlain fragrances and lit up in golden light. Adding to the decadent retail spaces, the building also houses a perfumed glove room, a Guerlain spa and the chic restaurant Le 68.

Cire Trudon

11 RUE SAINTE-CROIX DE LA BRETONNERIE, 4E

From the golden crest that adorns each of its products, to its range of candles made up in the busts of cultural figures, legendary candle maker Cire Trudon rarely strays from its French roots. Honouring the country's heritage, Cire Trudon's range of boutique luxury candles and scented accessories regularly references quintessential French wit. Cire Trudon has been in the business of making candles since it was founded in 1643 by Claude Trudon. Supplier to the House of Versailles up until the French Revolution and thereafter to Napoleon's imperial court, Trudon continues to ride the waves of fashion with high profile collaborations, recently inviting fashion designer Giambattista Valli to collaborate on a range. Its sumptuous beeswax candles find a fitting home in the Le Marais store on the winding street of rue Sainte-Croix de la Bretonnerie.

Le Bon Marché Rive Gauche

24 RUE DE SÈVRES, 7E

Staking its claim as Paris's oldest department store, Le Bon Marché has been catering to shoppers on Paris's Left Bank since husband and wife team Aristide and Marguerite Boucicaut started out in business in the mid-nineteenth century. Purchased in 1984, the store now operates under the LVMH (Moët Hennessy Louis Vuitton) group to bring shoppers everything they could possibly want from a high-end department store. Browse beauty and accessories on the ground floor, women's fashion on the first and second floors, childrenswear on the third and menswear on the lower ground floor. The original building at 24 rue de Sèvres was redesigned in the 1870s by the architect Louis-Charles Boileau and engineer Gustave Eiffel, giving Le Bon Marché shopping spaces a more intimate feel of boutique luxury. After renovating and refurbishing the building in 2015, Le Bon Marché unveiled a glittering shoe department under a light-filled glass ceiling in the womenswear section – the perfect showcase for its curated section of irresistible designer heels.

Van Cleef & Arpels

20–22 PLACE VENDÔME, 1ER

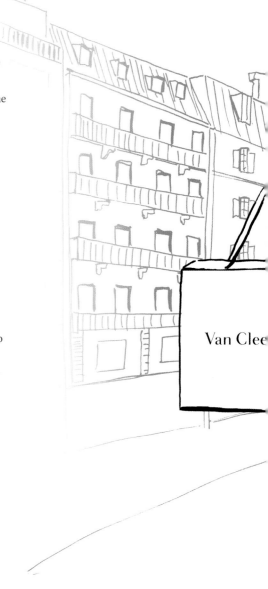

The glittering boutique on place Vendôme is the jewel in the Van Cleef & Arpels crown. As high-end jewellers of precious and semi-precious stones, Van Cleef & Arpels set up shop in the Parisian square in 1906 and still resides in its original premises opposite the Ritz. The store extends across a corner of the square and carries ranges of the house's fine jewellery, watches and fragrances, as well as offering bespoke services. There is even a school, L'École Van Cleef & Arpels, in the building, where students learn about the history and craft of fine jewellery and watchmaking. The Van Cleef & Arpels boutique was renovated in 2006 by designer Patrick Jouin, who transformed the store into the captivating retail setting it is today. Art Deco style is combined with feminine details like rose-shaped silver embossed wallpaper, gold leaf ceilings and crystal chandeliers, all of which are set against an austere palette of cream and white.

els

Schiaparelli

21 PLACE VENDÔME, 1ER

The influential surrealist designer Elsa Schiaparelli became known for her witty and eye-catching designs when she started out at the height of the Roaring Twenties. Mingling with members of the avant-garde, from Salvador Dalí to Man Ray, Schiaparelli is credited with bringing art into fashion. Revived some sixty years after the design house closed in 1954, Schiaparelli launched its haute couture on the Paris Fashion Week schedule in 2014 and today designer Bertrand Guyon resides as creative director. Behind its stately facade, the Schiaparelli store at 21 place Vendôme caters to its haute couture following with an exclusive salon as well as selling the house's range of accessories, including leather goods, silk scarves and jewellery.

Balenciaga

336 RUE SAINT-HONORÉ, 1ER

Balenciaga's rue Saint-Honoré store invites shoppers into a futuristic vision of fashion, with sleek lines that blend contrasting colours and materials. The interior was completed in 2012, in a renovation by former creative director Nicolas Ghesquière collaborating with French artist Dominique Gonzalez-Foerster. Coloured partitions divide the menswear, womenswear and accessories sections, and each of these features contrasting materials – vivid purple carpet, raw marble and traditional Parisian black and white tiles. The bold interior of the store honours its founder, Spanish-born Cristóbal Balenciaga, a master of minimalist couture who always looked to the future for inspiration. Today Balenciaga's creative director Demna Gvasalia continues the revolutionary tradition with designs that blend elements of high and low fashion in a new vision of the future.

BALENCIAGA
PARIS

Printemps

64 BOULEVARD HAUSSMANN, 9E

Now with two Parisian outposts – one in the Louvre and the other on boulevard Haussmann – Printemps was founded in 1865 and to this day prides itself on being at the fore of fashion. The iconic Haussmann department store is spread across nine levels that house menswear and womenswear, beauty, accessories and homewares. Come sale season, Printemps slashes prices on its designer wares, making it a must for fashion devotees. The showpiece of the historic interior has to be the jewel-like Art Deco stained-glass cupola that creates a light well over the arcades of the lower levels. The top floor is home to Brasserie Printemps, which offers diners panoramic views of Paris from the Eiffel Tower to Montmartre.

Maison Margiela
PARIS

Maison Margiela

13 RUE DE GRENELLE, 7E

Maison Margiela's rue de Grenelle boutique attracts Margiela followers to the Left Bank and the edges of the Saint-Germain-des-Prés district. Staff wearing white lab coats, the uniform of a luxury atelier, attend to shoppers within the store's austere retail setting. The House of Margiela's boundary-pushing mens- and womenswear is displayed in a space furnished with white covered furniture against a

Maison Margiela
PARIS

backdrop of trompe-l'oeil wallpaper. The conceptual setting reflects the way the House of Margiela has always bucked the trend of flashy fashion since being established by Belgian designer Martin Margiela in 1988. Margiela's design language favours a monochromatic palette that deconstructs fashion archetypes. After selling the brand in 2002 to Only The Brave, the holding company owned by Diesel founder Renzo Rosso, Margiela departed the maison in 2009 and has since been replaced by fashion provocateur John Galliano.

Debauve
& Gallais

30 RUE DES SAINTS-PÈRES,
7E

Every box created by chocolatiers Debauve & Gallais bears the regal gold crest of the maison – with the fleur-de-lis on an oval of its signature blue in the middle – and comes wrapped in a matching blue ribbon. Founded in 1800, Debauve & Gallais proudly stake their claim as makers of fine French chocolate for over 200 years. Visit their decadent store on rue des Saints-Pères on Paris's Left Bank to try the Pistoles de Marie Antoinette – an assortment of chocolate coins that honour the French queen. The story goes that the chocolate coins were created by Sulpice Debauve, the royal pharmacist, for Marie Antoinette to take with her medicine. The curved wood panel counter of the store showcases the irresistible range of chocolates that come in all shapes and flavours, from the signature truffles to the chocolate bonbons. You can make your own selection or treat yourself to one of the decadent gift boxes.

125

Céline

53 AVENUE MONTAIGNE, 8E

Opening in 2014, Céline's avenue Montaigne flagship builds on creative director Phoebe Philo's visionary approach to the female wardrobe. Artist Thomas Poulsen – who also goes by the name of FOS and with whom the house regularly collaborates – was commissioned to direct the interior design behind the historic Baron Haussmann facade.

The store features natural materials in unusual graphic formations: striking marble pillars, brass-lined shelving and pot plants gathered around a stunning curved staircase that connects the floors. The boutique stocks the brand's stunning womenswear, fresh from the catwalks of Paris Fashion Week, as well as the covetable range of Céline accessories and luxury leather goods.

Librairie Galignani

224 RUE DE RIVOLI, 1ER

The dark wooden shelves that line the walls of renowned bookstore Librairie Galignani house a curated selection of French and English titles. The story of Galignani goes back to 1520 in Venice, when the Venetian publishers were among the first adopters of the printing press. Moving the house from Venice to eventually settle in Paris, descendent Giovanni Antonio Galignani opened up shop on rue Vivienne in 1801. It was the first bookstore in Europe to specialise in books written in English. In 1856 they moved to their current rue de Rivoli address. The publishing house ceased at the beginning of the twentieth century, but the boutique bookstore shows little sign of slowing down. Its position in the heart of the first arrondissement – opposite the Jardin des Tuileries, under the gracious awnings of rue de Rivoli – attracts a steady mix of tourists, literary lovers and art-book connoisseurs.

Montaigne Market

57 AVENUE MONTAIGNE, 8E

Ever since opening boutique concept store Montaigne Market in 2005, founder Liliane Jossua has led the pack in luxury retail. With a curated selection of high-end womenswear designers from Paris and elsewhere around the world, Montaigne Market stocks established design houses along with some of the hottest up-and-comers on the scene. Names like Lanvin and Givenchy sit alongside emerging brands like Los Angeles–based Co and Japanese label Mame Kurogouchi. Montaigne Market has a thriving e-commerce store, but its original bricks-and-mortar establishment in the historic building on avenue Montaigne features a contemporary and monochromatic interior that functions as a sleek canvas for the designer mix on display. If you don't have enough time to visit all of the designer boutiques in the area or want to get up to speed on the latest fashions, Montaigne Market is *the* place to go.

Kenzo

**60–62 RUE DE RENNES,
6E**

Kenzo has been synonymous with colour and print ever since Kenzo Takada founded the label in 1970. The stores are no exception, bringing eclectic references together with a playful use of colour. With Opening Ceremony's Carol Lim and Humberto Leon now at the helm, the Kenzo name has been revived and brought into a new era.

The dynamic duo have established a reputation for themselves as retail savvy, keeping their fingers on the pulse with numerous collaborations and events that keep Kenzo at the fore of the fashion pack. From collaborating with artist Maurizio Cattelan on their in-house publication *Kenzine*, to producing a line for retail giant H&M, the Kenzo brand continues to diversify and flourish.

Lacoste

93–95 AVENUE DES CHAMPS-ÉLYSÉES, 8E

The story of the Lacoste brand begins with French tennis player René Lacoste, dubbed on court as 'the crocodile'. In honour of his nickname, René had a small crocodile logo embroidered on his sports blazer and it became his signature. After his retirement from the sport Lacoste partnered with André Gillier to start the company La Chemise Lacoste, which would later become the global high fashion sports brand it is today. Lacoste retained the sporting spirit of the Roaring Twenties, the era during which René rose to prominence in the tennis arena – when one thinks of Lacoste, one thinks of white polo shirts and tennis shoes. The brand continues to dress world-class athletes, attracting a global following and generating a spread of boutiques worldwide. The Paris flagship on avenue des Champs-Élysées won't disappoint, taking you from the street to the court as you step through the door.

<u>03</u>

Sleep

L'Hotel

13 RUE DES BEAUX-ARTS,
6E

Staking its claim as the smallest of Paris's five-star hotels, L'Hotel opts for an intimate boudoir experience across its twenty rooms. Formerly called Hôtel d'Alsace, the hotel was famously the last home of playwright, writer and dandy Oscar Wilde. L'Hotel honours its Left Bank literary heritage at every turn, from the interior – designed by Jacques Garcia – which is a homage to bohemian opulence, to the Michelin-starred dining venue Le Restaurant, which offers a tour and lunch dedicated to the famous author.

The boutique hotel is nestled in the fashionable Saint-Germain-des-Prés district, within reach of a selection of chic galleries, boutiques and luxury fashion. L'Hotel's spa and dining facilities will make it difficult to venture out, though. There is even an exclusive hammam pool and steam room where guests can unwind and maybe find a bit of creative inspiration.

Hôtel Plaza Athénée

25 AVENUE MONTAIGNE, 8E

Boasting breathtaking views of the Eiffel Tower, Paris's Plaza Athénée is located in the heart of haute couture with Dior's atelier only a few doors down on avenue Montaigne (*see page 66*). The ornate balconies of Plaza Athénée's historic facade are adorned with hanging flowerpots filled with red blooms, a setting that famously featured Carrie Bradshaw from *Sex and the City* during her brief sojourn in Paris. The colour scheme continues in the public spaces of the hotel with flashes of lipstick red across the seating and window awnings of the restaurants. A visit to the Dior Institut au Plaza Athénée (*see page 20*), the hotel's dedicated spa and treatment centre, is a must. Inspired by the classic modernism of the great couturier, it offers a rejuvenating venue for the fashion set that frequent the hotel.

The Peninsula Paris

19 AVENUE KLÉBER, 16E

From its stately facade to the hotel staff adorned in chic black and white uniforms, The Peninsula has been a mainstay on the hotel scene ever since the Roaring Twenties when it was called The Majestic and Parisian bohemians frequented the venue. Fast forward to 2014 and the building's current incarnation, The Peninsula, has retained many of the original Majestic spaces. Taking inspiration from haute couture, The Peninsula's luxury aesthetic can be found in every detail. A stunning glass installation, titled 'Dancing Leaves', by bespoke glass studio Lasvit graces the foyer, greeting guests as they enter the hotel's wrought iron and glass doors; the mix of historic elements and contemporary style is consistent throughout the building. Up on the rooftop, the hotel's terrace restaurant and bar, L'Oiseau Blanc, offers breathtaking views of Baron Haussmann's Paris and the Eiffel Tower.

Four Seasons Hotel George V, Paris

31 AVENUE GEORGE V, 8E

The building that houses the Four Seasons Hotel George V, Paris was originally constructed in 1928 in honour of the British King George V. In 1999 the Four Seasons moved in, creating a lavish eighteenth-century interior complete with tapestries, paintings and an eclectic mix of sculptures and objets d'art. Dining spaces, including a stunning marble courtyard, are lined with floral creations conceived by the hotel's artistic director and famed florist Jeff Leatham. Leatham's dedication to fashion has seen the hotel host a magical display of haute couture garments by Elie Saab during Paris Fashion Week in 2013; the venue's luxurious spaces provided a grand backdrop for the designer's sparkling creations.

Shangri-La Paris

10 AVENUE D'IÉNA, 16E

Built in 1896 as the private residence of Prince Roland Bonaparte, the botanist and grand-nephew of Napoleon Bonaparte, Paris's Shangri-La reflects its former owner's eccentric, stylish flair. Converted and opened in 2010 with a lavish interior designed by Pierre-Yves Rochon, Shangri-La Paris sits in the heart of Paris's haute couture precinct; just around the corner from the luxury shopping offered on avenue Montaigne, the hotel is a favourite of the fashion set. There are arresting views of the Eiffel Tower from many of the suites. The hotel's Michelin-starred dining and cocktail venues are also to haute couture standards.

Hôtel de Crillon

10 PLACE DE LA CONCORDE, 8E

Towering over place de la Concorde, Hôtel de Crillon has been a Parisian landmark since it was built in 1758. The building takes its name from its days as the private residence of the Count de Crillon. Transformed from private mansion into luxury accommodation in 1909, the hotel's stunning neoclassical facade mirrors the grandeur of Baron Haussmann's streetscapes and has witnessed Paris's turbulent history, from the French Revolution to the Napoleonic Empire. After four years of renovations under the watchful eye of architect Richard Martinet, the hotel reopened in July 2017, revealing an ongoing commitment to the building's history as an architectural and cultural emblem. With Karl Lagerfeld designing the decor of the hotel's two Grands Appartements, it was a highly anticipated event.

Le Meurice

Another highlight in Paris's suite of luxury hotels, Le Meurice has been pampering guests with five-star standards since it opened in 1835. Set on the grand rue de Rivoli and overlooking the Jardin des Tuileries, Le Meurice offers the crème de la crème in accommodation, from the opulent Louis XVI–style interior decked out with gilded mirrors and stately paintings to Philippe Starck's contemporary take on the hotel's spaces and restaurants. Salvador Dalí, who once frequented Le Meurice, is honoured in the Catalan-inspired menu of the hotel's Restaurant Le Dalí. Le Meurice's close association with culture and the arts extends to the Meurice Prize for contemporary art, created by the hotel and held each year to celebrate French and international artists.

Mandarin Oriental, Paris

251 RUE SAINT-HONORÉ, 1ER

Few five-star hotels can boast urban hives as part of their decor, but under chef Thierry Marx the Mandarin Oriental's rooftop garden is the home for a swarm of bees that supply honey to the hotel's Michelin-star dining and decadent in-house patisserie. The hotel's rooftop garden sits above the city of Paris with stunning views of the nearby Louvre, Jardin des Tuileries and place Vendôme.

Interior spaces are light-filled and airy, a less-is-more approach to decorating that suggests a classic understated elegance. The Mandarin Oriental is in the heart of the luxury fashion district on the boutique-lined rue Saint-Honoré. The hotel is also a short walk from many of Paris's most iconic landmarks and art institutions. Even so, it won't be easy to leave the inner city oasis of the Mandarin Oriental.

The Westin Paris – Vendôme

3 RUE DE CASTIGLIONE, 1ER

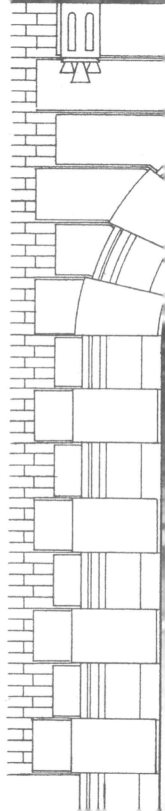

Taking its name from the iconic place Vendôme, the square Coco Chanel famously passed through to reach her atelier each day, The Westin is a popular destination for stylish travellers. Be enamoured of the hotel's sparkling gilt interior, particularly in the Napoleon and Imperial ballrooms, which are extravagantly decorated in the style of the Second Empire. Many of the hotel's suites offer grand views of Paris and the Eiffel Tower, and the hotel's fine dining and drinking venues won't disappoint. After wandering the boutiques of the district treat yourself to a cocktail at La Terrasse, the chic outdoor courtyard set off the hotel's Le First Restaurant; turquoise metalwork adorns the courtyard, which features a central fountain, offering the perfect setting to relax in after a day of shopping.

THE WESTIN

La Maison Favart

Nestled in the theatre district of Paris, La Maison Favart prides itself on its quaint boutique character amidst Paris's luxury hotel offerings. The hotel is named after its former residents – the glamorous Favart couple who worked at the theatre institution the Opéra-Comique, which is just a few steps away. And in their honour the interior is decked out in extravagant eighteenth-century style. Decadent rococo wallpaper depicting provincial scenery offers a theatrical backdrop for the carefully curated selection of furniture and art objects adorning the hotel's intimate interior. It's an eclectic mix that doesn't shy away from colour: splashes of red, purple and blue bring a contemporary twist to classical French style.

Saint James Paris

43 AVENUE BUGEAUD, 16E

Located in the sixteenth arrondissement on Paris's Left Bank, Saint James Paris is a delightful surprise when entering off avenue Bugeaud. Built in 1892, the hotel reflects its history, blending predominantly Second Empire styling with various aspects of subsequent design periods. Get lost in the quirky details like zebra busts, playful illustrated wallpaper, extravagant chandeliers and plush velvet upholstery that make the interior a rich visual wonderland. For an opportunity to pamper yourself, Saint James Paris's exclusive Guerlain Spa is not to be missed. The spa continues the hotel's boudoir style, fusing eastern and western influences with ornate detailing. It even boasts two Turkish baths.

Le Royal Monceau, Raffles Paris

37 AVENUE HOCHE, 8E

When it opened its doors in the 1930s, Le Royal Monceau was frequented by the city's creative coterie: the flappers, like Josephine Baker; the fashion icons, like Coco Chanel; and the artists, like surrealist Man Ray. Today the hotel balances these bohemian roots with a contemporary twist thanks to Philippe Starck, who was entrusted with the renovations the hotel undertook in 2010. Describing itself as an art hotel, Le Royal Monceau blends Art Deco style with high art, housing its own cinema, gallery space and art bookstore – La Librairie des Arts. The hotel remains a favourite for the glamorous set visiting Paris, particularly during Paris Fashion Week.

Ritz Paris

15 PLACE VENDÔME, 1ER

Once the private residence of Coco Chanel, the Ritz Paris continues to uphold luxury standards when it comes to accommodation. In honour of the designer, the Ritz's longtime guest, you can treat yourself to a night in the Coco Suite, the room that Mademoiselle lived in and decorated herself. The room reflects Coco's classic palette of cream and gold, with splashes of black lacquer and the designer's beloved emblem: the golden lion.

Even the hotel's dedicated spa and treatment centre, Chanel au Ritz Paris (*see page 30*), honours the designer with a menu showcasing the Chanel beauty range, including the famed Parfum No. 5. This Belle Époque hotel was also a favourite of Paris's literary circle: other former guests include F. Scott Fitzgerald and Marcel Proust. It is hard to resist the Ritz's gracious charm.

Le Bristol Paris

112 RUE DU FAUBOURG
SAINT-HONORÉ, 8E

In 2016 I had the honour of becoming the artist-in-residence at Le Bristol Paris. It's where I always stay when I'm in Paris and I proudly consider it my (very glamorous) Parisian home. Located in the heart of rue du Faubourg Saint-Honoré's high fashion district, Le Bristol Paris has upheld the district's ritzy standards since it opened in 1925. Its owner, matron of France's high-end hotel industry Maja Oetker, oversees the creative direction of the hotel in every detail. Under Oetker, Le Bristol Paris's sumptuous interior reflects its luxury credentials.

In eighteenth-century style, spaces are filled with decadent touches, from the antique furniture and gilt chandeliers to the ornate floral motifs repeated throughout the soft furnishing in the private rooms and public spaces.

The hotel also boasts a Michelin-rated repertoire of fine dining, which includes Eric Frechon's Epicure restaurant (*see page 200*) and Café Antonia (*see page 196*). No wonder the hotel has been, and continues to be, a favourite of the glamorous set, like silver screen actress and fashion icon Rita Hayworth and the many fashion designers and photographers who frequent Le Bristol today.

Hôtel Costes

239–241 RUE SAINT-HONORÉ,
1ER

R enovated by Jean Louis Costes and
Jacques Garcia in 1995, the hotel's
Belle Époque-meets-boudoir styling gives it a
distinctively bohemian feel that extends from
the hotel's public spheres to its private spaces.
But it's as a bar that Hôtel Costes has forged
its reputation. The celebrated cocktail bar
occupies the ground floor and oozes attitude
with red-lit corridors and irresistible cocktails.
The luxurious dining setting also regularly
attracts the fashion industry's in-crowd, from
Victoria Beckham to Beyoncé, making Hôtel
Costes worth a visit for a decadent drink and
some celebrity spotting.

04

Eat/
Drink

Angelina

226 RUE DE RIVOLI, 1ER

Paris establishment Angelina's irresistible hot chocolate has been drawing crowds since it opened its doors in 1903. Counting Mademoiselle Coco Chanel a fan (the designer used to frequent the Parisian teahouse), Angelina continues to hold institution status and now has a global presence. Angelina is positioned opposite the Jardin des Tuileries on rue de Rivoli and, upon entering, you'll find yourself transported in time and space to the days of the Belle Époque. You won't be able to resist the menu of extravagant pastries and sweet treats, from the luxurious Mont-Blanc – a recipe of meringue, cream and chestnut paste vermicelli – to the humble classic, the chocolate éclair. For me, though, there is nothing quite like their thick and creamy hot chocolate on a chilly winter's day in Paris. Now with outposts from Tokyo to Dubai, Angelina has become a worldwide success, bringing a little taste of Paris to the rest of the world.

The Restaurant
and The Terrace

HÔTEL COSTES, 239–241 RUE SAINT-HONORÉ,
1ER

Get lost amidst the velvety candlelight and seductive atmosphere of Hôtel Costes's dedicated dining venues, The Restaurant and The Terrace. Designer Jacques Garcia, together with the hotel's founding brothers Jean Louis and Gilbert Costes, has set the scene with an opulent Napoleonic interior.

The playful but irresistibly chic Costes sensibility continues in the menu, which serves up French brasserie classics with a twist, like black angus grilled filet with bearnaise sauce. My favourite dishes on the menu are spicy lobster pasta and their famous cream cheesecake. The Costes institution is abuzz during Paris Fashion Week. Pay a visit and rub shoulders with the fashion and art clique that frequent the venue, like fashion 'it' boy Balmain designer Olivier Rousteing.

Ralph's

**173 BOULEVARD
SAINT-GERMAIN,
6E**

It's no secret that Americans love Paris, ever since the days when literary expats like Ernest Hemingway and Ezra Pound frequented the Left Bank. Ralph's – another American in Paris – sits above the flagship Ralph Lauren store on boulevard Saint-Germain, in an irresistibly elegant seventeenth-century building that continues to welcome local Parisians and visitors alike. The cafe reflects Ralph Lauren's modern simplicity, from its interior to the menu's repertoire of American classics such as the lobster salad and Ralph's burger. Dishes arrive on gold-edged plates inscribed with 'Ralph's'. One of their sweet touches is that every coffee comes with a mouth-watering little bowl of salted caramel popcorn. The venue's warm wood-panelled interior combines high-end dining with the designer's quintessential ranch-style elements in a setting that continues to draw in an overflow from Paris Fashion Week.

Café de Flore

172 BOULEVARD SAINT-GERMAIN, 6E

Nestled in amongst the irresistibly chic galleries and fashion boutiques of boulevard Saint-Germain, Café de Flore has been a Parisian institution since it opened its doors in the late nineteenth century. Occupying a street corner, the cafe's tables that spill out onto the pavement are the perfect vantage point to take in the street style of the glamorous shoppers making their way from boutique to boutique – it's my favourite spot in all of Paris to sketch chic Parisians as they walk by. One of Paris's oldest coffeehouses, the iconic venue was famously frequented by Left Bank luminaries like the dadaists, including Tristan Tzara, and existential philosophers Simone de Beauvoir and Jean-Paul Sartre. The cafe continues to serve up classic Parisian fare and coffee to the art and fashion set, making it an industry favourite; when visiting Café de Flore, you might find yourself brushing shoulders with Jean-Paul Gaultier or Karl Lagerfeld as you sip a café au lait.

Cristal Room Baccarat

GALERIE-MUSÉE BACCARAT,
11 PLACE DES ÉTATS-UNIS, 16E

H oused in the extravagant Galerie-Musée Baccarat, the mansion that is the former residence of Marie-Laure de Noailles, the Cristal Room Baccarat is one of the most magical dining experiences Paris has to offer. With architect Philippe Starck commissioned to renovate the space in 2003, the Michelin-rated restaurant combines old and new. Take high tea surrounded by the sparkling crystals that adorn the walls and hang from the ceiling – an awe-inspiring chandelier of one hundred and fifty-seven glittering lights makes for a stunning centrepiece. Diners can book a decadent thirteen-metre-long Baccarat table, lit up from its crystal base, for a truly luxe dining experience.

Brasserie Lipp

151 BOULEVARD
SAINT-GERMAIN, 6E

BRASSERIE

Opened in 1880 by Leonard Lipp and his wife Pétronille Lipp, Brasserie Lipp is a Parisian institution that has attracted members of the Left Bank's cultural clique since its founding days. The interior features ornate tiles, painted by Léon Fargues, that depict exotic plants and are staggered across the mirrored walls. The ornate wood-carved fixtures and the brasserie's varnished mahogany facade are quintessentially Art Nouveau. Describing themselves as a 'shrine to Parisian gastronomy', Brasserie Lipp offers classic French dishes, from blanquette de veau to tarte tatin. Dishes are delivered to the table by waiters in white shirts and bow ties. The venue has been a favourite of celebrities and fashion cognoscenti, like Madonna and Kate Moss, and is a popular setting for exclusive parties during Fashion Week.

Bar Le Dokhan's

117 RUE LAURISTON, 16E

Bar Le Dokhan's stakes its claim as the City of Light's first ever Champagne bar. Set in Le Dokhan's hotel, the bar has a menu that showcases more than two hundred Champagnes. Sip well known names like Dom Pérignon and Moët-Hennessy, or try some of the boutique and vintage finds, sourced during the head sommelier's regular visits to the Champagne region. Bar Le Dokhan's gilt and green baroque-style interior is as sumptuous as its sparkling menu. Ascend to the bar in the stunning elevator made from a vintage monogrammed Louis Vuitton steamer trunk – and enjoy a glass of red in style.

Bar Hemingway

RITZ PARIS, 15 PLACE
VENDÔME, 1ER

I n his memoir about the city, Ernest Hemingway wrote, 'Paris is a moveable feast'. Named after the great writer, Bar Hemingway at the Ritz lives up to this line in every sense. Enjoy a menu of the most exquisite cocktails Paris has to offer in honour of the American expat, from a Serendipity to an Old Fashioned. The extensive cocktail and drinks menu has been put together by expert bartender Colin Field. Once frequented

by the likes of Cole Porter and F. Scott Fitzgerald, the
bar is once again back in business, reopening in 2016
after renovations. The wood-panelled leather interior
is decorated with photographs and memorabilia of
Hemingway; even a metal cast of the author's head sits
in the corner of the bar. The cosy, saloon-style setting is
perfect for a Parisian nightcap.

Pavillon de La Fontaine

JARDIN DU LUXEMBOURG, 6E

C reated in 1612 on Paris's Left Bank, and an initiative of Queen Marie de Médici, the geometric footprint of the grand Jardin du Luxembourg takes inspiration from Florence's baroque Boboli Gardens. Set amidst its charming manicured lawns and numerous white marble sculptures, the Pavillon de la Fontaine is the park's dedicated cafe and the perfect respite from wandering the greenery. Take a seat at a table under the dappled shade and, with a coffee in hand, enjoy some excellent people-watching. Observe stylish Parisian families, ambling tourists or the chic art and fashion crowd drifting in from the nearby Saint-Germain-des-Prés district.

Pavillon de La Fontaine

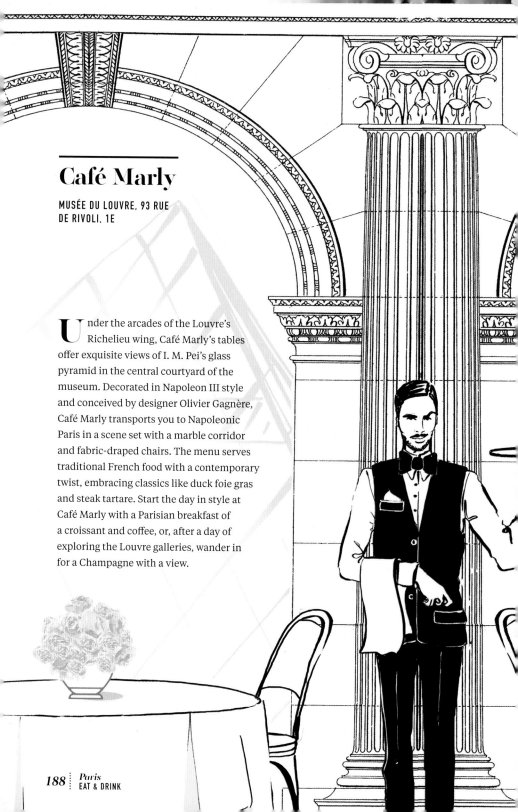

Café Marly

MUSÉE DU LOUVRE, 93 RUE DE RIVOLI, 1E

Under the arcades of the Louvre's Richelieu wing, Café Marly's tables offer exquisite views of I. M. Pei's glass pyramid in the central courtyard of the museum. Decorated in Napoleon III style and conceived by designer Olivier Gagnère, Café Marly transports you to Napoleonic Paris in a scene set with a marble corridor and fabric-draped chairs. The menu serves traditional French food with a contemporary twist, embracing classics like duck foie gras and steak tartare. Start the day in style at Café Marly with a Parisian breakfast of a croissant and coffee, or, after a day of exploring the Louvre galleries, wander in for a Champagne with a view.

L'Avenue

41 AVENUE MONTAIGNE, 8E

O ccupying the street corner of avenue Montaigne and rue de Marignan, L'Avenue is the perfect pit stop between the designer boutiques of Paris's eighth arrondissement. With Dior (*see page 66*), Chanel and Céline (*see page 126*) just a few steps away, it's no wonder the venue regularly attracts a cast of star-studded clientele. Outside, the cafe's tables spill out onto the sidewalk; whereas inside, amidst the plush red velvet seating, L'Avenue offers a warmly lit atmosphere. Headed up by famed restauranteur and hotelier Jean Louis Costes, who, along with his brother Gilbert Costes, has been responsible for a selection of trail-blazing venues and fashion haunts around Paris including Hôtel Costes (*see page 166*). The menu reflects a dedication to French cuisine, making L'Avenue the perfect Parisian post-shopping destination.

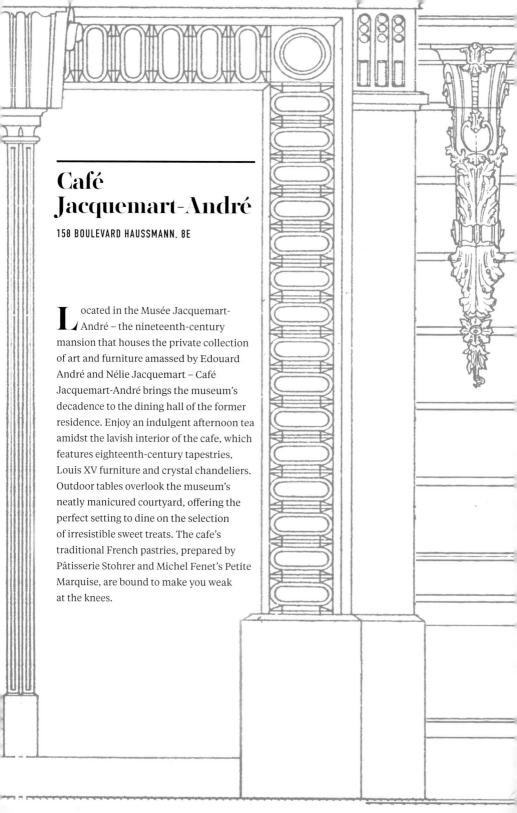

Café Jacquemart-André

158 BOULEVARD HAUSSMANN, 8E

L ocated in the Musée Jacquemart-André – the nineteenth-century mansion that houses the private collection of art and furniture amassed by Edouard André and Nélie Jacquemart – Café Jacquemart-André brings the museum's decadence to the dining hall of the former residence. Enjoy an indulgent afternoon tea amidst the lavish interior of the cafe, which features eighteenth-century tapestries, Louis XV furniture and crystal chandeliers. Outdoor tables overlook the museum's neatly manicured courtyard, offering the perfect setting to dine on the selection of irresistible sweet treats. The cafe's traditional French pastries, prepared by Pâtisserie Stohrer and Michel Fenet's Petite Marquise, are bound to make you weak at the knees.

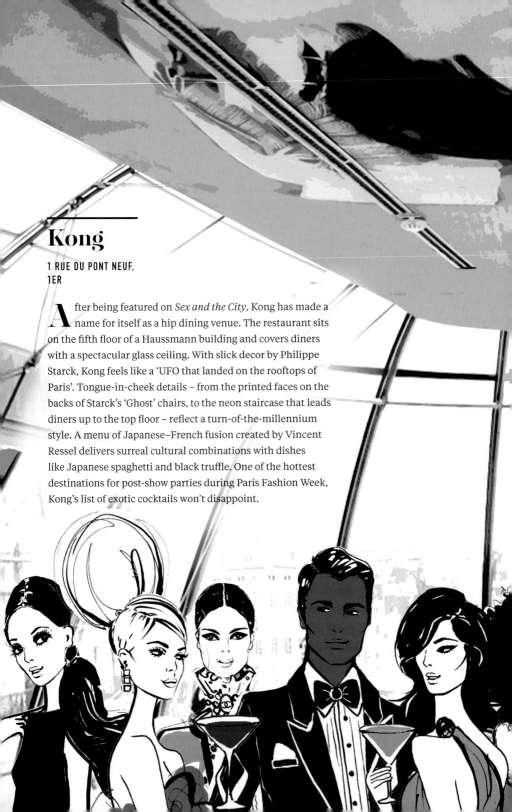

Kong

1 RUE DU PONT NEUF,
1ER

After being featured on *Sex and the City*, Kong has made a name for itself as a hip dining venue. The restaurant sits on the fifth floor of a Haussmann building and covers diners with a spectacular glass ceiling. With slick decor by Philippe Starck, Kong feels like a 'UFO that landed on the rooftops of Paris'. Tongue-in-cheek details – from the printed faces on the backs of Starck's 'Ghost' chairs, to the neon staircase that leads diners up to the top floor – reflect a turn-of-the-millennium style. A menu of Japanese–French fusion created by Vincent Ressel delivers surreal cultural combinations with dishes like Japanese spaghetti and black truffle. One of the hottest destinations for post-show parties during Paris Fashion Week, Kong's list of exotic cocktails won't disappoint.

Café Antonia

LE BRISTOL PARIS, 112 RUE DU FAUBOURG SAINT-HONORÉ, 8E

Taking its name from one of history's most infamous sweet-tooths, Marie Antoinette, Café Antonia reflects Le Bristol Paris's decadent side. A portrait of the French queen overlooks the sumptuous brocade-adorned interior of the patisserie and salon de thé, which are located on the ground floor of the hotel. The decor is ornate and chic, taking its influence from the rococo style of the queen who loved the finer things in life. Head chef Eric Frechon and pastry chef Laurent Jeannin serve a menu of breakfast, lunch and dinner, but it's at high tea that Cafe Antonia truly inspires – a selection of sandwiches, scones and petits fours arrive on tiered cake-stands, along with a selection of fragrant teas or, as Marie Antoinette would have it, a glass of Champagne.

Laurent Dubois

2 RUE DE LOURMEL, 15E

Fromage connoisseurs need look no further than Laurent Dubois's extravagant cheese emporium. Opening his original store in 1996 on rue de Lourmel, and now in three Parisian locales, Laurent Dubois has established his name as a leader in French cheesemaking by winning the prestigious Meilleur Ouvrier de France award. The revered fromagerie celebrates France's cheese history.

Dubois sources his extensive range of cheeses from local producers, bringing the cheeses to the city to mature at the Laurent Dubois headquarters. Sample some of the decadent varieties on offer that reflect the country's thriving cheese industry – the luxurious Comté and Camembert make crowds flock to the boutique.

Epicure

LE BRISTOL PARIS,
112 RUE DU FAUBOURG
SAINT-HONORÉ, 8E

Describing itself as the 'defender of French cuisine', Epicure takes itself seriously. Headed by Eric Frechon, the Michelin-rated restaurant is a gastronomical wonderland that lives up to this grand promise. From purple sea urchins to black truffles 'cooked with underbrush aromas', Epicure's seasonal menu is the dining equivalent of haute couture. My favourite part of the dining experience at Epicure is the custom-built mirrored dessert cart displaying the most incredible sweet creations you will ever see. Located in the luxury hotel Le Bristol Paris *(see page 164)* – a venue that is no stranger to the chic celebrity and fashion crowd – Epicure's serene baroque-style decor is pure elegance. During the summer months the restaurant spills outside into the gardens, offering a delectable experience in the hotel courtyard.

1ER.

2E

3E

4E

5E

6E

7E

$c\mathcal{A}$cknowledgements

—

To Meelee Soorkia, our fourth book together and as always, I am so incredibly grateful to have had the joy and privilege of working with you. You are and always have been the best editor an artist could dream of. We've built a beautiful little collection of books together and one lasting friendship!

To Laura Gardner, thank you for all the research you did into this book. Your persistence and genuine love of Paris has made every single detail all the more beautiful in this book.

To Martina Granolic, you are the only person in the world who knows exactly what I'm thinking without me even saying a word! Thank you for being by my side through every single step of creating this book and putting so much love and attention into this and everything you do.

To Murray Batten, I now consider you 'The Book Design Whisperer' and it never ceases to amaze me how you can make text dance across the pages and bring my illustrations to life! I'm so grateful to work with you.

To Justine Clay, thank you for encouraging and supporting my work from the very beginning. I will still be thanking you when I'm 100 years old because without you I would not have the career and opportunities that I have today.

To my husband Craig, I fell in love with you long before we ever went to Paris but it was on our first trip there together that I realised that we'd be together forever. Thank you for encouraging every single little and big dream of mine.

To my two children, Gwyn and Will. You make me the proudest mum in the world. I love you both more than the hundreds of stars that shine above the Eiffel Tower!

About the author

—

Megan Hess was destined to draw. An initial career in graphic design evolved into art direction for some of the world's leading design agencies. In 2008, Hess illustrated the *New York Times* number one selling book *Sex and the City*, written by Candace Bushnell. She has since illustrated for Dior Couture, created iconic illustrations for Cartier and Louis Vuitton in Paris, dreamed up animations for Prada and Fendi in Milan, and illustrated the windows of Bergdorf Goodman in New York.

Hess's signature style can also be found on her bespoke limited edition prints and homewares sold around the globe. Her renowned clients include Chanel, Dior, Fendi, Tiffany & Co., Saint Laurent, *Vogue*, *Harpers Bazaar*, Cartier, Balmain, Louis Vuitton and Prada.

Megan is the author of four bestselling books and the Global Artist in Residence for the Oetker Masterpiece Hotel Collection.

When she's not in her studio working, you'll find her sketching in a cosy corner of her 'home away from home' at Le Bristol Paris.

Visit Megan at **meganhess.com**